I GRADUATED NOW WHAT?

10 Strategies
To Survive Life After College

BRANISHA HOLLIS

TABLE OF CONTENTS

ACKNOWLEDGEMENTS

To the one that can see my struggles coming before me. To the one that I can talk to about anything. To the one that designed me for this very moment. I say, thank you. Please continue to hold my hand through this blessing called life. I appreciate the handhelds thus far. Thank you to all my dearest family and friends who has helped me through the hard and happy times that I spoke of. To my grandmother, Rosia Sue Walker, - look at me now ☺ May you rest in peace with no pain.

INTRODUCTION

Wow! Where do I begin? Sunday, May 17, 2015 marks five years since I graduated from Clark Atlanta University. God was good then and he is still good now. I've gone through new problems, tests and trials but managed to pull through. In another five years I'm sure there will be a new set of problems, tests and trials, but guess what; I'll pull through those as well.

After college I was able to visit my dream place; Japan. I was able to study abroad the summer after graduation and found out about this opportunity at an information session that I'd attended the fall before Christmas. I didn't have any job offers, so I figured, why not? Anything that I needed to take care of could wait until I got back from the best six weeks of my life thus far. This was my big chance and I was not about to miss it.

Taking care of things once I got back home was not easy however. I knew it wouldn't be, but who really thought it'd be so hard? I went a whole six months without a job offer after I applied everywhere. All I kept hearing was that I was too qualified. Of course, those weren't jobs in my field but they seemed to be hiring. To tell you the truth I didn't want them either, I just really wanted to get my foot in the door somewhere so I could build on my knowledge and network so when it was time for lights, camera, action, I'd be ready. I wanted to do my own thing first and then be creative in my field with my own company. Yes, I majored in mass communications with a concentration in television. Yes, I was capable of the behind-the-scenes work and on camera. Did I want it now? No. Did I try and try to get hired in my field? Yes. I didn't apply like I didn't want it. As a matter of fact, you couldn't even tell that I didn't want it.

Regardless of whether I wanted those jobs or not I wasn't going to get them anyway because the economy was not my friend. I couldn't even get a fast food gig; no one would hire me. So I took matters in my own hands and said, "Okay, let me just go back to school and that way it's not like I'm out here not doing anything." On the other hand, let's not be fooled, THAT REFUND CHECK WAS GOING TO HELP ME OUT! No shame in that at all. I mainly went back to school for the refund check. I didn't want to be in grad school, I could have cared less about a master's degree. I'm more of a hands-on person and all school was doing those days and times was holding me back. Nevertheless after a while I quit graduate school. I gave it a year and decided to throw in the towel because I was not feeling it. School had no meaning and added no value to my life, I wasn't making a difference and I wasn't happy. School wasn't rewarding, which meant I couldn't be inspired by it, or inspire others, which is what I feed off of. I was starving but couldn't eat because there was no food a.k.a. inspiration for me. Applying to jobs was the same as it was when I started. Now I was not only jobless but school-less as well. When you can't have what you want what are you going to do about it? When giving up seems to be near what will you do? This book is designed to help you with life after college and the challenges that you'll face along the road to success.

— TURN THE PAGE! —

CHAPTER 1

Seek No One's Approval But Your Own

"The great majority of men and women are not original, for they are not primary, have not assumed their own vows, but are secondaries-grow up and grow old in seeming and following; and when they die they occupy themselves to the last with what others will think, and whether Mr. A and Mr. B will go to their funeral."

Emerson [1841]

1. Don't Make Decisions Based on Your Current Emotional State

When we tend to make decisions based on our current emotional state at the time, they're usually wrong, rushed, and/or eventually uncomfortable. Decisions as such can become regretful and even leave you feeling ashamed of yourself.

I spoke with a co-worker today who just graduated in May and because of his current state he isn't making any effort to further his search for a job in his field. He's too busy hating his current job and letting others who don't have degrees dictate to him what his future should look like. Remember, he recently graduated in May and it's now September. We had a nice conversation about what transpired from then untill now. I came to the conclusion that he had no fight. I said, "Boy, where is your fight?" He just looked at me. Then he said, "Branisha, I don't know. I need your help." By the end of our conversation he'd told me more of what he hasn't done while telling me all that he had, which brought me to the conclusion that he hasn't really done any real work to better his situation.

Guys and girls, men and women, please don't waste too much time. There will be time wasted because that's just what usually happens but don't waste too much. How do you think you're going to feel after all that wasted time? Where is your fight? My co-worker lost his fight way too soon; don't do that. Have the fight attitude and if you don't have it, find a way to GET IT.

Since then I'm happy to announce that my co-worker is currently waiting to hear back from a company concerning a job in his field. I'm so happy because this is what he's been waiting for. He just needed to refocus his mind and figure out what he really wanted out of life. He needed to not seek anyone else's approval about his goals and most of all, he needed to let go of making drastic career decisions when he was feeling lost, hopeless, confused and overwhelmed. I'm definitely a victim of this strategy because I too have been faced with some tough decisions at times in my life when things weren't so favorable.

Once upon a time while in college I made a decision that would have affected the first four to eight years of my life after college. I didn't' want to but I figured I'd adapt. I knew I could manage it, but deep down I didn't want to.

By now, you either got the hint up top or you're still wondering what it is. Here it is; I joined the Air Force ROTC Officer Program my sophomore year in college at the school I was currently attending. Every Tuesday and Thursday evenings, aside from PT (Physical Training) days, I was Cadet Hollis. Every day that I had to go was a day that my power was stripped away from me. I made that decision based on what my mom and grandfather wanted. There were other facts that contributed to this desperate decision as well.

My grandmother passed so I was doing whatever made sense to everyone else while trying to look on the bright side of things. After that emotional moment in my life had passed, I took my power, personality, and perseverance back. My drive was unmatched.

While the ROTC program was stripping things away from me, it also taught me about things like core values and physical fitness. I got a chance to meet students at other schools in New Orleans but none of those things were the point. I do appreciate the things that it taught me, but I couldn't make that a permanent move for my life. I made a decision with all the wrong kinds of feelings and for a good reason overall but for the wrong reason for me. Which is why to this day I don't understand the concept of settling.

Settling doesn't sit well with me at all. It can be hard to keep my composure when I know someone is doing so. A prime example was described earlier when I talked about my co-worker. He was just going to settle for what life had to offer after only being a college graduate for four months. It's not even just about settling for jobs or the current state you're in, I'm talking about settling for PEOPLE too.

Let's be real here—not for a second but throughout this entire book. People make up a large part of our feelings and encompass "the what and why" of how we're doing things. Whether it is a parent, a friend, a boyfriend, a girlfriend, a roommate, or a co-worker.

If you are around settlers then you my dear are in with the wrong group of people. If that boyfriend or girlfriend is blocking your *go*, then *he or she* must go. You will not be happy and treat others right, including yourself, if you're not happy about your own life.

Also surviving life after college can make you vulnerable and open to a great deal of insecurities. Don't date the wrong person because there's nothing else to do or because you feel like you need to feel wanted. Don't make that kind of decision at any point in your life. When you do, you lose focus on what really matters at the time and you don't even think about ways to get out of what you're in anymore, because now the focus has changed. Sometimes when the focus changes to a big distraction like that it leaves an opening for settling.

Now here is something big you should really listen to:

DON'T LET OTHERS SETTLE IN YOUR LIFE.

Usually when a book is being written or when it's a talk from me to you type of thing, you are always the victim. I mean after all, we are talking about YOU and how YOU can survive this life, right? However...

What about you bringing down someone else's survival? What about you letting others settle in your life?

Your life is happy and theirs isn't and not only are you not feeding them what they need to be better, you're letting them settle in yours so you'll have someone or so you won't be alone. This goes for any kind of relationship. Relationships are all around us and we have multiple ones in action all the time but there shouldn't be any kind of settlements going on.

Don't mistake being in a job that you don't currently want as me saying you're settling, that's not settling. That is you doing what you have to do right now to make it and get to step two. Settling is when you give up on what you really want or don't want to work for, because you've grown lazy and gotten too comfortable where you are so you figure you might as well stay where you are. There are other excuses as well like your age, health, disbeliefs, and discouragement. You don't think your goals are attainable anymore because you've heard the word "NO" too many times. Those are all just current feelings to down you some more and deter you from what's yours.

2. Know Your Options

Do you really think about any other option after college other than getting that dream job or that job to survive until that dream job comes along? I'm going to guess that you probably don't. Or you might say you're going to do something, but don't really know how you're going to get it done. At times I think we end up doing what we need to do versus what we want to do. Trust me, I understand. In time that can lead to always putting needs versus wants first when it comes to your career and dreams, which is very detrimental for you.

I didn't have a big job or any job for that matter lined up after college so I gave myself the option of doing something that I've been anticipating since middle school; I went to Japan.

How did I do that? Well, at the beginning of my senior year, I went to the study abroad office to get details on the process. I discovered that at Clark Atlanta University you can still study abroad after graduation but only for the summer. I got all the information that I needed in order to plan and prepare. I knew trying to go to Japan any other way would be expensive so I used my university to my advantage. I applied for scholarships and I knew I was getting refund checks for both semesters so I calculated the amount I needed to save to pay for the program. I

My room in the girls dorm

also took generous donations from anyone who wanted to help. My mom and aunt, who both were in the military, also helped me with my plane ticket and money to have in my pocket while there. Yes, I'm blessed but I still had to find a way or make one which is what I did.

So Japan was the option I gave myself right after college but what about when reality kicked in once I got back? That's when it came hailing down on me with the struggles. Unfortunately I didn't have luck with getting jobs anywhere so I was forced into going back to school, which I hated, for a master's degree. I needed something to do and a way to get money and school was the answer.

From the introduction you already know that didn't last so what was a girl to do?

Finally after researching and praying I decided that it was time to explore the option of teaching overseas in another country. This wasn't the first time this option had presented itself.

I previously considered doing this right after college with a colleague of mine, but it would have been in Korea. We had a previous classmate in the graduating class before us go so that's how we knew about it. I was so stuck on my original plan before that-going to Japan for study abroad, that I couldn't fully give my attention to it. Plus my mom was in the Navy on deployment and I would have had to leave Japan, go home for two weeks and then head directly to Korea. That wasn't enough time to spend with my mom who had been gone for eight to nine months. Money was also a serious issue as well.

Of course you don't have to guess where I picked to go; I couldn't wait to go back to Asia to my glorious Japan! My teachers were trying to get me to stay to teach when I went the first time but that wasn't good timing for me. As I mentioned above seeing my mom played a factor and I wanted to see what my other options were. I wanted to try other things.

One of my main goals was trying harder at being a songwriter. Things were looking a little better for a while but it wasn't as big an opportunity as I wanted. I was actually proud of myself for getting from one point to another with it. I was hanging out in home studios more while meeting other writers and music producers which was a big deal to me, I was now actually writing to music not just the tunes and arrangements I heard in my head. And while nothing became official it was more than I ever did so I gave myself a pat on the back. Although it didn't work out then that's still a passion of mine so I won't stop with it. I will always go back to that because it is part of my heart and it's another way to help people.

I knew it was time to teach abroad, when I was hit with a very low point in my life. I already knew which two companies that I had to choose from so all I had to do was choose. I needed a drastic change and what better way to start that change then somewhere totally new.

Before we get into the rest, let me say this:

I SAT BACK AND PRAYED ABOUT MY SITUATION. I WAITED TILL I WAS AT PEACE TO FURTHER MY DECISION TO TEACH IN JAPAN. THEREFORE I DID NOT MAKE A DECISION "IN MY CURRENT EMOTIONAL STATE."

I know you're probably thinking that Japan wasn't as new to me as it sounds but it actually was. Although I'd been twice before I went to teach, each time I learned something new. The second trip gave me an opportunity to explore two different parts that I'd never visited and I took the bullet train further out than I was used to. It was one thing for me to visit for a few weeks but to make Japan my home for a year and pretty much going where I would be staying on my own was a whole new chapter.

I was so nervous to make the move but ready at the same time. The application/hiring process took close to three months so I was

on pins and needles. Sure enough, I got the callback and was head over heels for my new beginning. Getting that phone call was like a breath of fresh air; I was going to Japan to teach and it was definite. Finally I thought to myself, I have something to add onto this life after college. I had something to work towards and be proud of at the same time. It wasn't about others being proud of me; it was about me being proud of me.

Now consider your options. Know what they are or what they can possibly be, keep a list if you need to. Write them on sticky notes. Remember to not seek any other approval but your own. It's your life and the have and should have songs are old and tired.

If there is something that you're seeking and it requires certification or a license, then go get it. If it's a skill that'll help you provide for yourself until infinity then do it.

CHAPTER 2

Work Doesn't Start or Stop With a Nine to Five

"Sometimes You Don't Know Why You Have To Wait, Until You've Waited To See Why You Had To Wait."

– Branisha Hollis

3. Have a Skill

I'm sure there are so many wonderful things about all of you who are reading this book and once again I thank you and I'm very grateful.

BUT...

Give me something more than what textbooks taught you or tried to mold you into. What skills do you have? What skills do you want? What skill do you admire that you've seen in someone else you've encountered?

I'm sure there are some things that you've said you could do but never really thought about doing. Perhaps there are a lot of things that you can do but never saw them as a way to make income. If none of those things are true then maybe you're seeking a new way to make money through a license and you enroll in a class to get the certification and began working.

Before going further let's examine ourselves to see what our personal skills are. What is it that you do best as a person? What are some of the characteristics that you carry with you everywhere, regardless of the job or situation?

For instance, I'm a people person. I'm helpful, friendly, talkative and bubbly. If you know who you are then that can be one way to factor in what you might want your skill to be. That's if, of course, you don't already have one.

For example, some people are just naturally great at doing hair, but don't think about doing it on the side for extra cash. If that's you, then go for it and manifest that skill. You may be able to even go get a certificate or license to be able to stretch that skill further if need be. I'm not one of those that was blessed in that category; my friends and I joke all the time about my future daughter suffering because I can't do hair. Styling hair as a stylist, beautician, hairdresser, or barber is a popular skill set to have if you can do it.

Since I can't, I decided to get my bartending license. I knew I was getting one more refund check so I thought, okay Branisha, what good can you do with your money that will benefit you other than going shopping or doing something that wouldn't last or help your future? I had been saying I wish I was a bartender and that I thought I could do that job. My people skills are dynamic and I have a great personality. I knew the skills that I possessed went perfectly with that job. I just needed those drink mixing skills.

Now if you know me, which some of you don't, you know that I don't even drink enough to know anything about what alcoholic beverages mix well with others. On the other hand, I wasn't totally lost either. Just because you don't drink a lot doesn't mean you can't bartend, but if you are totally clueless, then you should go out, listen and watch people; then you can do it.

I will admit that I was a bit nervous because this was something totally new and on top of that you're sitting in the course with professional drinkers or people who have alcohol-mixing experience. There were a number of people in my class who already served at clubs and restaurants so they wanted to further their future businesses or careers. If you have some serving experience on top of having a bartending license you'd make a great hire for some lucky employer. Speaking of serving, that's another great skill to have. I also did that as well.

At numerous places you have to serve food first before they let you behind the bar, especially if there isn't enough experience as they see fit. They want you to know the menu, get a feel for their customers and their drinks. I understand the concept but it can still be frustrating depending on the place that you apply to. Now back to bartending...

DRINK RECIPES - HIGHBALLS

Highball is a term used to denote drinks made with liquor(s) and juice(s) or soda(s).

PROCEDURE

Glasses will vary in size from 7-9 ounces but will have a high ratio of soda or juice to the liq makes for a consistent taste in the drink.

Be ___ re to fill the glass completely with ice, this contributes to the consistency of the drink. If t en ___ ice, the drink will be weak, as more soda or juice is needed to fill the glass.

LIQU ___ SODA / LIQUOR & JUICE	EXAMPLE: VODKA & T ___
1. Highb ___ s filled with ice	1. Highball glass filled with i
2. 1 oz. of L ___ Bourbon, Vodka, Whiskey, Gin etc.)	2. 1 oz Vodka
3. Fill with so ___ r or juice	3. Fill with tonic water
4. Garnish when ___ d	4. Garnish with lime wedge

TERMS USED WITH HIGHBALLS

DOUBLE: When a cus ___ requests a double, use 2 oz. of liquor, then fill with soda or ju double the cost of the dr ___ Dewars and water costs $4.25, a double Dewars and wat $8.50.

SPLASH: When a customer re ___ drink with a "SPLASH", then you would use a roc of a highball glass and just add a s ___ of the requested juice or soda.

TALL: When a customer requests ___ "TALL", use a Collins glass or larger bever customer is requesting a weaker tasting ___

EASY ICE: When a customer requests a ___ ASY ICE", the customer wants a weak ut in the usual size glass the drink is served

LOAT: Some highball drinks call for a liqueu ___ er ingredient to be "FLOATED". m needs to ___

Server from 2012-2015

I found a class online that seemed to be popular and on the plus side had a location in Atlanta, so I checked it out and filled out paperwork. Those classes were fun and intimidating as well. Although my people skills are dynamic, when you're a fresh bartender, you need to make sure you can talk while making a drink at the same time. People see us and think that it's simple and that they can do it but if you're not used to dealing with a crowd of people while making an Oreo Mudslide or a Mojito, then you can sink in your own sweat. That's something very different from making a Crown and Coke and then calling it a day. Ultimately I'm thankful for my bartending and serving skills.

Notice that I chose my skill from what I'd been admiring and my people skills, but what else?

MONEY.

I needed a hustle that was going to produce money for me quickly. I knew bartending would send me home with money daily regardless of how much it was. I needed daily money and I'm not a trap girl so I couldn't get it from there. I wasn't going to strip although I kid every once in awhile about doing so.

Hey, I KNOW YA'LL CAN RELATE TO HAVING SOME CRAZY THOUGHTS WHEN THINGS AREN'T GOING RIGHT FINANCIALLY IN YOUR LIFE.

Needless to say, let your skill be one that helps you produce some extra income. Even if it's not daily money, it's still something. What you previously read was what I wanted and needed to do. Everybody can't bartend or serve food so whatever it is that you can do, just do it. Get your skill. Get your money. Get your hustle on.

4. Be a Hustler

Each shoe signifies a job

We are just going to jump right into this strategy because it is very self-explanatory. If you want it, go get it. If it takes you having a billion jobs to get to your big picture and/or to satisfy your present being then by all means necessary; HUSTLE.

By now my friends know my two favorite words and they are hustle and green. Those two words go together very well for me. I'm still going to hustle regardless of the matter, but why should you hustle? Why do people hustle? Everyone has their own reasons but I'm talking about the why of when you really want something.

That making-my-life-a-better-fit-for-me-to-live why. That I'm-going-to-make-it-one-way-or-the-other why.

You see I graduated from Clark Atlanta University and the things that were instilled in us were to always get what we want. If they won't give you a job, then make your own. When something is missing and you're a graduate of Clark Atlanta University, you be the voice and fill that void. You are never scared and you "Find a Way or Make One."

After being taught that and having that instilled in me, I couldn't just sit around moping about not having a job or not having the job that I wanted. I had to do what I had to do. I didn't seek anyone's approval. I knew my options while finding more and lastly, I got myself a skill that would make me extra income aside from what I was getting or didn't have to start with.

Right now I have three jobs. I can tell you that it isn't easy, but it's going to be worth it in the long run. I tell myself that every day. Although I'm thinking about putting in a two weeks' notice at one of them right as I'm typing this, I still know that I'm willing to do whatever it takes. I humble myself and tell the Lord that wherever I have to work, I'll do it.

It. Is. Hard. Out. Here.

Not every day is the best day but I make it work. It sucks leaving one job and going to the next and meanwhile neither of them are paying/dishing out what you want. Bartending can be satisfying but when it's slow, it's slow and yes, it does depend on where you work. Right now I'm bartending, working at an athletic shoe store

and I'm a paraprofessional at an elementary school. You have to do what's best for you. You have to see what is waiting for you on down the line in your future. You determine how far down the line is and when you're going to get there. I'm doing my absolute best to get there as fast as I can, with prayer in between, on top, under and on the side. Life can slow you down but don't let it get in the way and stay there.

Please don't think because I have three jobs means that you have to copycat. I won't even be able to say that in about another week or two and it hasn't even been that long being at my third job. What I did was recognize early on that it wasn't worth it, because of my hours at the school. On weekends I'm really trying to be at the bar for sure, so I had a decision to make. It was a hard one to make too, because when I say I'm going to do something for a certain amount of time, or once I put it down in my plan, I go through with it. I'm loyal to it. I couldn't be loyal to this plan, it didn't fit into what I had going on.

In the beginning things were fine because I was applying to work full - time at the athletic shoe store and was going to work part-time at the bar like I already do. I humbled myself because I needed to make more money so I didn't care that the hourly rate wasn't over $10 anymore. Thankfully while I was at the athletic store doing my new hire paperwork, the principal of the school where I'm working now called and offered me a job. Yes, there were some praises going up to the Lord, because I needed that stability check.

There's nothing wrong with having numerous jobs or hustles if you can handle it but everybody needs that one stable check that's going to save other things in your life from crumbling if the side hustles aren't cutting it by themselves. Despite that I decided to keep my athletic store job which was a bad idea, I know I mentioned the hourly pay wasn't worth it and it wasn't, but the other main reason was my TIME.

How was I going to write this book and put time into my other business if I'm always at work for somebody else? Not to mention being totally exhausted some days after dealing with kids who I love dearly.

However, if you pick your jobs right, that won't happen. After all, this strategy is called be a hustler, but just be a smart one. Pick jobs that go together with your time and any other factors that are important to you. For instance, although I'm quitting my athletic store job, I'm waiting on a car service to check my background so I can begin that. The hustle doesn't stop, but it will get smarter. It'll get better and it'll start to make more sense.

Make sure your one hustle or multiple hustles make sense for what you need and for your time. They need to be worth it.

My hustles must allow me some wiggle room. I need to be able to come and go as I please. I need a lot of flexibility but it might be different for you.

I was even going to start selling hair or wigs but I found out that I didn't have the funds for it but mostly I discovered that I liked wearing hair and wigs more than I liked to sell them. Everyone is doing it now too so I'll pass unless my creative juices start flowing.

Overall I'm proud of myself. I humbled myself and the Lord opened up another door. I just have to keep it moving while keeping myself inspired and encouraged. I know you can do it too. Remember to design things around you, not around what somebody else is doing. It needs to all work out for you and your schedule.

5. *Update Your Resume*

While all the hustling and new skill sets are being created please be sure to update and make multiple resumes. I have a newer version of my resume with jobs I've held on it and I have one specifically for bartending that includes where I worked as a server as well since they go hand in hand. Always document where you've worked with new job descriptions. You never know when an attractive position will come available. If you don't already have a resume for it then you might miss it.

You want to keep things as professional as possible. I used to carry my resumes around with me for just-in-case situations. I kept them in a manila folder in my car.

There have been plenty of times when I didn't have my resumes with me and wished I had. Even if you don't keep them in your car, take them with you if you know you're going to a certain city or event where you'll meet people that are possibly hiring for jobs you're looking for.

A word of caution; the in-car strategy could be a bit unsafe because your personal information is on your resumes, so just be careful and only carry them when you think you'll need them. Also always have them in your email to send to someone right away if the need arises. Send yourself every copy of each resume that you have so it'll be easy to get them to the right person quickly. In this age of technology, timing is everything.

Even if you aren't skilled at writing resumes, that's a poor excuse not to have one version or multiples. Either someone can help you craft a good one or you'll just have to pay for the service. I paid someone to do mine and she did a stellar job. I was too desperate for a new one and didn't have the patience to try to do it myself and mine needed a serious update at the time.

Please understand that just because you have a great resume doesn't mean that you will always get the job or that yours won't be set aside because of what's on it. I've heard of this happening but never experienced it firsthand myself until someone else looked at my new, pretty resume.

A man looked at my resume and said it still needed some work, but he only really put emphasis on two things; my name and the school I graduated from. Of course I was very defensive about both. I was amazed by the fact that this really happens. He suggested that I use my middle name and abbreviate my first.

I know he was just trying to help but the thought of being discriminated against before I even had a chance to get an interview blew me away. I was hoping I'd get to talk to him but that never happened so I let it go. I brought this up just so anyone reading this will be aware. If it ever happens to you and you know why, then I hope you handle it well. My advice would be to pray and keep it moving. Regardless of race, name, gender, or what school you attended, it may not be the first or last time you're discriminated against about something whether you know or not. Chances are high that you don't want to work with people like this anyway.

CHAPTER 3

Love Who You Are, Love Where You Are

"If God comes a second too early, it won't be the right time. The Lord has a record for being an on-time God for a reason. He will come in due time, due season."

Min. Marcus Taylor

6. Don't Be Embarrassed

Before writing about this strategy I sat and asked myself if there was a time at any point on this journey where I became embarrassed about what I didn't have. I don't recall a time when I was, I do recall maybe thinking people were embarrassed for me. It could have just been in my head, but sometimes the way people looked at me when I said where I worked or didn't work was strange. Sometimes it's as if they expected me to be doing better.

To be honest, I expected me to be doing better too but that wasn't the case and at least I had a job. You really have to excuse people and the way they think or perceive what or how you're doing. Luckily I never cared about what someone thought I should be doing. To me I was always working towards something bigger and better anyway, whether I knew what it was or not. Never lose sight of the fact that there is no shame in any kind of honest work even if it's not really what you want in the long run.

When the struggle is real you need to have thick skin. People's actions and words can really hurt when you're in your time of need and wanting something more.

When it came to certain things in my life I've never been society-based. Being society-based will leave your butt hurt. Things that you must do to make it cannot embarrass you. I applied for jobs I was told I was too qualified for which is just stupid to me still. I applied to McDonalds and I had a friend apply at Burger King and neither of us ever heard anything back from them. We laughed about it till we were in tears but kept it moving. It never occurred to us to be embarrassed at all.

If you are a person who is embarrassed about having a degree but working somewhere that is supposedly "beneath" you then please get it together and be thankful. All the energy you put into being embarrassed can be used towards getting out of your situation. If you know you're better than that then do something about it!

Honestly sometimes being embarrassed about where you are in life, whether it's your career or life status, can stem from insecurities brought on by other people. For instance, if you're in a relationship and you're content with your situation and at first your partner was too but then changes their mind, that can lead to you being embarrassed. Don't let that happen to you either. Everyone has his or her own journey of how this life process works. If that person can't be down with you before you can get back up then he or she can get the exit too.

Instead of complaining about where you work or if you're trying to change it, he or she should be helping you by sending you jobs from online postings and filling out applications for you while you do others or while you're at work. I don't mean that he or she should do all the work but helping out not only encourages you but gives you a safety net of them being really down for you.

In situations like this you have to talk about what's at hand and communicate to the best of your ability. Times are different and you darn near have to be as creative about finding a job as you do with the job once you're in it. Remember that people are on this journey with you and just as your skin needs to be thick, so does theirs. Every once in awhile you'll have to tell them how to treat you or treat someone else who is looking down on you.

What it all boils down to is that the people who are on the journey with you know what's up. They know how long you've given yourself to be in that place and they know the hard work you're putting in to keep yourself encouraged. So when you are and aren't around they should be another force that you have to fight off negative and nosey people.

Family isn't off the hook either. Sometimes our parents can tend to think it's about them when it really isn't. They can sometimes forget to separate themselves from the equation and how they feel about what's going on with you.

Now my mom hasn't necessarily done this because she knows her child, but she will talk about what I have done already and I told her that she doesn't have to do that. She doesn't have to worry about what anyone thinks of me because we got this. Yeah I'm her child and she doesn't want to have the slightest feeling of someone giving off negative energy towards me but that's how it is sometimes. We just have to smile and keep it moving. I have to cover my mom in prayer because she will go off on people about her Branisha. My mom plays no games when it comes to me and I'm thankful for that when it's the right time.

My grandfather can sometimes put his feelings all in the mix too and trust me, I know it's out of love and care, but just like my mom, he has to trust my process too and know that those prayers he and my grandmother prayed are already coming to pass. He is so quick to tell me about teaching jobs, which are his first choice for me, and when Delta was hiring for flight attendants, he liked that too. He just knew I was going to hop on that, but I didn't. He knew trying to get me to teach was like pulling my leg but he still tried.

Speaking of that matter about me teaching, let's discuss being embarrassed. What about being embarrassed about what you didn't do, or what you settled for? I know I've touched on settling in a previous strategy, but is settling something to be embarrassed about?

Ever since I came back from Japan and even before I went that's all I heard. Teach this or teach that and it got and still gets on my nerves now. Teaching would be a settling job for me. It's like when there is nothing else to do and no one will hire you, everyone suggests teaching. If that's what you want to do, then be my guest. For those that don't want to, don't let anyone pressure you into it.

Granted right now I am a paraprofessional for a prekindergarten class. I'm not however the main Jane in the classroom and it's prekindergarten. I said if I ended up on a school's payroll it would only be as a paraprofessional. I didn't even want to be a substitute which I know now is what I should have been doing because it pays well.

I feel some people tell themselves that they're going to teach for a year or two and then get stuck in it. I never wanted to be that person. I'd be trying to save every child without when there's more to focus on at hand. Not even just that, though. Teaching is something I never wanted to do. If I'm going to teach you anything being confined to a classroom all day isn't how I'm going to do it.

My grandfather and I have been back and forth numerous of times about that teaching position. What I don't understand is how can I take away a position from someone who's been dreaming about doing that forever? There are people out there looking to be hired who have a passion for teaching but they can't get the job because I'm settling for it and don't really want it. That was always my go-to when I was talking to him about this subject.

I'm not in any way knocking being a teacher. I know people who are great at it and love it. What I am knocking is settling when you know that you don't want to. That energy can go somewhere else.

Do I love my job right now? Yes I do, and I love those kids, but is it something I see myself doing long-term? No, it isn't. Even for this job, I went through months of not hearing anything after I applied. Honestly, it was a last act of God type of thing. It found me versus me looking for it. While I'm at it I'm going to enjoy it and all of its perks, like being off for holidays and still getting paid in the summer.

What about those perks though? At the end of the day, are those perks going to keep me happy for the rest of my life? Will I let them blind me from what I really want? The answer is no, because I don't want to look back on this one day, talking to my kids about what I really wanted to do versus what I did and how I didn't try hard enough to do it. I don't want to tell them I settled for anything. To me that's embarrassing.

7. Be Happy for Your Colleagues

This particular strategy is one of the most important ones in this book. They all hold importance and their own weight, but this one can break you if you're fragile. I can honestly say that I have been happy for each and every person I graduated with who has done anything that he or she wanted to do. However, when everyone else is moving on it can be hard to watch when you feel like you're not going anywhere.

There was one particular time when I was having a bad day about my life. I became aware of a friend's accomplishments and afterwards they gave me the feeling of envy for a while. I'm very happy to say that the particular feeling didn't come first or last long, but it came.

After seeing their accomplishments I was so happy for that person, I mean super happy, but after that hype of happiness, I wished I had what I saw. I had to check myself and not beat myself up about what I didn't have. I also had to check myself about wanting exactly what my friend had.

You have to be very careful about wanting what someone else has because you never know what he or she had to do or sacrifice to get it. You never know what people are going through while they're in it. There are a lot of people who enjoy showing you what they're doing, but when they go home at night, their prayers are a different story. Let what they did or are doing inspire you but not because of envy.

I'm so glad that it only happened to me once because I'd never want the Lord to think that I wasn't happy for the next man or woman. I can't block my blessing and you can't either. It's coming you guys, I promise that it is but you have to remember what I said here in these strategies. You have to dream, work and plan. You really can't do one without the other; it doesn't work like that.

So when you see someone who has put his or her work and prayers to the test, rejoice together. Pray that he or she keeps a clear head in the game. If you're close to him or her check on them to see how it's going.

I have plenty of talks with some of my friends who are succeeding right now and I tell them all that my time is coming. We encourage each other and we look out for one another. There is no envy.

When I say let it inspire you, you should do just that. Let that big announcement or new career move from someone else make your drive even harder. Let it make you get up off your butt and do something to further whatever it is that you want. Get your plans down on paper, fill out that job application or go to work with a better attitude knowing that it's only temporary and you'll be in a better place soon.

It's so easy to let what you see break you and make you give up instead of inspire you, because of all the new social media outlets that we have. I'm not going to blame it entirely on social media because you have to grow a protective shell that'll protect your emotions from going haywire. The intentions of people posting their happy times or success isn't meant to make you drink yourself to sleep or have negative feelings. As I stated above let it give you a positive outlook.

Switching to another topic but sticking to the same strategy of being happy for your colleagues, let's touch on marriage and kids. Think back to when you first said, "I'm going to get married one day and have kids." How old were you? Did you understand what it was that you were saying? I ask those questions because usually when we say those things we have no clue as to what it takes or have even thought about where we would be in life when that time comes.

I think this is important to talk about because there are too many people letting their age tell them when to do things. I've had some girlfriends that have been sad about turning 26, 27 and 28 without having kids and a husband. They secretly envy other women who already have them.

If you don't have at least more than half of your buckets in a row, that should be the last thing on your mind, male or female. How can you envy someone else who has all these things that you don't have when they have already figured out who they are and where they're going? You don't have the right to be mad or sad about someone else supposedly having your dream life and you don't even know what the next step in your career is. I'm not saying it shouldn't be perfect at some point, but you don't want to make things more frustrating. You don't want painted pictures of someone else's growth and happiness in life.

Stop letting society and other people's pictures script you about what to do and when. Some people are moving too fast. Don't be that person caught up in moving too fast; enjoy life, travel, brand yourself, and everything else will come, but you must make sure that you make time for it. If it's already there and someone is rocking with you through all of this then hey, you guys set your own timetable while in the meantime, get it together, be happy for others and move on.

8. Seek Help

Since I've been on this journey after college I have become way more humble than I already was. I have had to reach out for help from others, but I didn't want to. Reaching out for help was hard, because I've always been the helper and the giver. I love to help and to give, but it was almost like the Lord was saying, "Branisha, I'm going to put you in a place where you have to ask for assistance. You will have to ask for favors." I was not too big on letting others help me because I honestly never had to before.

It wasn't even a matter of pride; I didn't even think that it showed a sign of weakness. I was simply just used to finding a way myself. I only leaned on my immediate family for help and that was mostly financially. As things started to change I found that I needed help with more than just that. I needed ears to listen to me vent. I needed friends to cheer me up when I was having a bad day; I was in need of a lot of things.

I needed to reach out to people that worked for employers that were hiring or just some ground advice on ways to go about doing certain things. Even though this next story that I'm about to tell happened my senior year of college, I think it's still fitting here.

It was a cold day in December and we had finals. It was also my birthday week, which always came around that time. I was hitting some hard times financially. My friends knew because we all were, but of course, I wasn't always as clear as to what was specifically going on or about what I needed. All that week I had been riding around on my gas and I knew eventually I'd need more but I didn't know how I'd get it. My mom provided me money not too long before but it was gone. I decided not to work my senior year so I could enjoy it but that wasn't the best idea as I soon discovered.

By the end of the week it was my birthday and I had no plans and no money. I also didn't have any gas. I went to my friend Jaralyn's apartment which is where my friend Britney and I sometimes stayed to avoid driving all the way back to where our families lived. I was just trying to give myself some fresh air and a nap before I asked anyone for more money. When I woke up, somehow Britney and Jaralyn got me to go to my car. They were trying to go somewhere and I was trying to figure out how to say, "Look, y'all, I don't have any gas for this surprise, or whatever we're doing." So we all got in the car and I cranked it up. When I cranked it up, I saw that my tank was almost full. At the same exact time, I was looking crazy and they were saying happy birthday. I immediately started crying. I was so shocked at how they played it all out. They were up to no good while I was asleep. To this day in the year 2015, that was the best birthday present ever. It was thoughtful and sincere and most of all it came from real love. We still laugh about it to this day.

The beauty of that story is that I didn't have to reach out for help because my friends knew that I needed it and that's what friends are for. Sometimes you don't have to reach out, people close to you can see a silent cry and it helps if they have an idea of what's going on. They knew they had to be as sneaky as possible because I would have turned their money down just as quick as the blink of an eye.

In conclusion don't be afraid to ask for help when you are in need. It will not hurt you to ask, the answer will either be a yes or a no. If you know someone in the line of work you want to go into then ask for advice on how you can gain entry. There's no way you'll be able to function in this world without a little bit of help from someone. I've learned my lessons and I'm writing this book to help you with yours.

9. Don't Let Yourself Go

In the midst of all that you're going through—the doubts, confusion, struggles, trials, etc., don't ever leave the house looking how you feel. If I was at home looking poorly then it definitely wasn't reflected in my appearance once I left the house. Many see it as putting on a show for people. They think it's you portraying that you have it all together. It's not any of that, at least in my opinion. There's nothing wrong with not looking like what you are going through and what you've been through.

No one wants to see the beaten down version of you, no one wants to see a pity party. How would you explain walking out of the house looking a mess to the person who controls that job you're trying to get? You never know whom you might encounter on a down day. A resume isn't just a piece of paper; it's your physical appearance as well.

I've mentioned a couple of times here that my senior year of college was rough in many ways. One of the issues was that I gained so much weight. My health seemed to be fading, I wasn't breathing the same and I couldn't sleep. I did research and read about things that could be causing all my symptoms and it was definitely me being overweight.

Pictured with the same person 4 years apart. On the left was in 2010 which is the year I graduated from college and she high school. On the right was her college graduation in 2014. Major weight changes for me.

I let myself go in that area and was so caught up in everything else that I didn't even see what was going on with my health until those symptoms came. I knew I wasn't eating and living healthy but it wasn't as important as everything else at the time. So if that's you right now, please change your habits.

Don't you want to look good for that new job and new phase in your life? Don't you want to be able to look a certain way once you get what you want? You don't want to have to catch up to anything; you want to be on point with everything. If you have extra time then your body, mind, and soul are good things to focus on. During grad school and after I quit my job, exercising is all that I did. I didn't have a job and until the two internships that I did have I decided not to sit around my apartment eating and moping around. So if this applies to someone, get up and groom your appearance.

10. Keep God First

I saved the best for last! Before you even read the rest of this, just close your eyes and really ponder on what the Lord has done for you. I might have hit some nerves with some of these topics and you may remember what you did or didn't do. Try to dig deep and feel his presence.

Keeping God first is going to be the start of anything new and old. It's a strategy that doesn't fall in place at numbers two, six, or seven. It has to be above everything that you think is the finest. When people lose hope and faith in you and when you lose it in yourself, God is still rooting for you. He sent his son to help you and me through so we can live.

None of this, and I mean absolutely none of this would be possible without him. Actually looking back on it and all those times I wondered, "Why me?" and I'm sure the Lord was up there thinking, "Girl, I'm preparing you for a book; a book full of your stories and strategies to help people the way that you helped yourself." I can laugh now, because it was rough. It's crazy too because out of all the things that have happened and didn't happen, I've had someone who has never left my corner.

To this day some people don't realize that's the difference between God and man. He is literally always there. He is the real MVP, not me and not you. Maybe you've had some flashbacks of your own reading some of the things that I said because something similar happened to you too. Did you glorify Him during the good and bad? Do you now understand what was going on? Do you see why you had to go through what you went through and maybe are still going through?

Some days all I had was the promising word of the Lord. Some days I would get so fed up with nothing happening. It was like I was in battle with myself. Have you ever been so down that there was nothing anyone could do or say to make you feel better? God can make you feel so much better and He's worth it. Every day that He wakes us up, He's telling us that we're worth it and we have another shot at making it happen.

Guys, I know it gets hard out here. Even though I'm writing this book and praying that it helps and reaches so many people I'm still following these strategies. I'm still working towards the life that I want to have for my future family and myself. Honestly I'm sitting here debating about putting in another two weeks' notice. Day in and day out I'm weighing the whys and the why nots. Some days it's still hard for me, I still have loans that have skyrocketed. My aunt cosigned for them which put her at a disadvantage financially and that puts me in a certain place financially as well. I really have to get out here and make some things shake. When I sit and think about what all she has done and still is doing for me, I cry and get sad but God is and God does. He has blessed her for helping me. I only pray that I can do the same and write one big check one day to her and Chase student loans. I got Sallie Mae in there as well.

The point is, I've tried to be as real as possible in this book. I didn't want to use any statistics or quotes from other known people throughout this. All of the quotes are from real people that I know except for the one quote in the beginning. I designed this book to help you mentally and honestly it's helping me as well. If anything, I have to give God even more glory. Telling some of my little stories took me back into those old feelings and into that time when things weren't always the greatest. Despite that, I think I turned out pretty well.

Just remember that you're going to need that extra strength, little push, soft hug and love. God will be the one to give it to you. By all means follow the strategies because they are what you need to survive but you also have to change your mental state. If your thoughts are completely negative, there's no way you're sleeping at night, at least not peacefully. Change the way that you think, change your mindset.

I love each and every one of you reading this book. I pray that you succeed in all that you're doing. I pray that you receive help from the right person or people and that they change your life for the better. I pray that if the devil gets to you even for a hint of a second, that you turn that thing right back around.

Know who you are and whose you are because I do.

Remember, work doesn't start or stop with a nine to five. You have to work before nine and after five, so let's get to it!

I love you.
Peace.

"Doesn't matter what people saw you do last night. Doesn't matter what someone heard you say yesterday. It's about your spiritual being. Your physical being will never be right. Get out of the flesh; it reminds you of your struggles, sickness, and heartaches." – My pastor, Rev. Eddie F. Collier of Towaliga County Line Baptist Church.

Dear Branisha

Dear Branisha,

I recently graduated Fall 2015 from Clayton State University. I first attended Gordon College majoring in Communications from 2009-2011. I transferred to Clayton State University Spring 2012. I decided to change my major after attending Clayton for one semester. My hopes were to be a news reporter, but then I changed my major to English. Many asked me what I was going to do with my major and even I was uncertain, but my heart led me to change my major. My grandparents were not happy about my decision at first because they wanted to make sure I was certain. I was very ready to finish college because it seemed like I had been in school for so long. I attended college for six years when many people finish in four years. I refused to give up on my dream of finishing school and making something out of myself. I am the first child for both of my parents to attend college and graduate. A lot comes alone with attending college, working, and being a mother, but nothing could stop me from reaching my goal. Many fears arose through the years that haunted me and made me push harder and sometimes too hard.

One main fear that haunted me was me thinking that I was not going to find a job. I was uncertain about exactly what I wanted to do with my degree up until the beginning of 2015. I decided that I wanted to work in the school system and potentially start teaching within a year. I was very nervous about my decision at first, but once I saw a job opening in the Griffin/Spalding County School System I took time and applied. So to state the least, I got the job and I am currently a Pre-K Paraprofessional. I plan to be in my own classroom the beginning of the next school year.

People always ask me how I did it, and I say, "Nothing is too hard unless you allow it to be." I started college when my daughter was four months old and now she is seven. Some people said I would not amount to anything, but look at me now. If you never give up on your dreams and continue to push, no one can stop you from reaching the top. God made all this possible for me and kept me strong.

Dear Branisha,

A big house, an awesome marriage, beautiful healthy kids, and my dream job... That was how I envisioned my life after graduating from college. I just knew that once I received my degree, I would be ready to take the world by storm. I had my entire life planned out. I would graduate, settle in my career, get engaged, get married, and start a family. Life was going to be great! The saying "if you want to make God laugh, tell him your plans" comes to mind as I think of how my life has gone in a totally different direction from the life that I envisioned. Finding a job was extremely hard. It seems like almost every job that I applied for required 2-4 years of experience. It took me almost a year to find a job, and it still wasn't in my field. I decided to go back to school to get a master's degree, hoping that it would provide better opportunities. Today at the age of 25, with a bachelor's degree and a master's degree under my belt, I am still searching for my career. I know that my career, along with everything else that I've ever wanted is on the way! You can never be fully prepared for life after college, but taking every experience as an opportunity to grow, building your resume, and learning to be thankful will take you a long way.

Ashley
Clayton State University

Dear Branisha,

Believe or not, life after college for me is where my most ultimate struggles to strive for success began. Like most people, I felt like because I had overcame tremendous obstacles in my life and still graduated with my Bachelors degree that everything would be smooth sailing from that point on, but to my surprise I was in for a very rude awakening. There I was, a fresh college graduate with a beautiful newborn baby staring me in my eyes. I had my precious baby girl exactly 2 months after graduating from college. I had been looking endlessly for jobs, turning in resume' after resume' and still no luck. I had it all planned out. I was going to have a job before my baby arrived. I just knew that I would be a competitive applicant because I had a Bachelors degree. Unfortunately that was not how things unfolded. There I was 3 months later, with a baby, a degree, and no job. I felt like I had failed although I had accomplished one of my goals, a goal that many people don't succeed. I felt like giving up, I felt like I had wasted 4 years of my life, and I felt like I had let down all of the people who believed in me. I was literally at my lowest point when God sent me a revelation. One day after I had been praying and crying and praying and crying constantly asking God "what have I done so bad to deserve this", these words came to me, "You can do all things through Christ who strengthens you". At that very moment I knew what I was missing, I realized that I couldn't give up, if I had never fought before this was my time to really strap up my boots and fight until the end. I had a reason and a purpose to fight for. It wasn't just me anymore, now I had this precious little life that depended on me. I had to realize that I had to keep God first. He was the one who gave me the strength and knowledge I needed to achieve my goals anyways and as soon as I obtained I put him on the back burner. That's what I had been missing. I didn't keep God at the head of my life. I let life's ups and downs cause me to lose focus on the one who had brought me through so many different trails and tribulations. At that point I became refocused. Instead of using the single parent lifestyle as an excuse, I used it as fuel to keep me going. I was determined to overcome any statistical analysis about single parents and career failures. Being a single parent made me fight twice as hard although it wasn't easy. I just had to keep pressing on. Now shortly 3 years and 7 months later I am still fighting and don't plan to stop until I make it all the way to the top. I have been an educator for 3 years now, I have a Masters Degree, and in 4 months I will be graduating with a Specialist Degree. So my encouragement to others who may find themselves in similar predicaments as myself is don't let your current situations determine your final destination and remember you can do all things through Christ who strengthens you.

Sincerely,

Corendishe Watts

Fort Valley Alum

Dear Branisha,

I was having a difficult time trying to recall how I felt after graduating college. There were a series of emotions I went through, a feeling of accomplishment to finally have my degree after attending three schools and changing my major twice; fear because now it's time for me to enter the real world. I had expectations to find a job in my field which ended up being a disappointment. Ultimately making me feel as if college was a waste of time or the only option to not feel like I was failing at being an adult. So I enrolled and become a student again, which I did (twice) and ended up regretting. I'm not so sure what I expected college to prepare me for, but this life I'm living is far from what I imagined. Sometimes I struggle with the current status of my life, because I had hopes and expectations that my degree would catapult me into a career track in my field of study. I think if I were given the option to do it over again I would go a different route with college right after high school being last on that list.

Sincerely,

Elle

Clayton State University

Dear Branisha,

After receiving my degree in mass communications I was thrilled and ready for the real world. Well... that all changed after I realized I had to move back home. That was a bomber because I was use to living on my own in college. After graduating I started looking for jobs in my field. It was a struggle for about three years. I had part time jobs, I thought about going to the military, I had Sallie Mae on my back, and I was starting to become frustrated. I started to second guess myself. I started to believe that I was a failure. I had a degree and I wasn't using it. Thinking back, I probably was slightly depressed until I started to pray. My prayer was the same everyday. I asked God to show me the way and open doors that I couldn't open by myself. Currently, I'm working in production as a sound engineer. I'm no where near where I want to be but I'm closer than I was three years ago. With that being said, don't give up, be patient and pray. Things don't come over night just like graduating didn't. It takes time so buckle up and enjoy the ride we call life.

"The real fun doesn't start until after you graduate "

- "B"

CAU alumni

Dear Branisha,

College.

I went in for my sentence for about a year and a half before I was released, mainly due to being a victim of a racial hate crime, but that's besides the point. lol.

Currently, i'm not in school.

The year and a half that I was there was bitter-sweet. Real bitter and real sweet. It was only an hour away from home, but it was in the middle of no freaking where. Our school made up 60% of the towns population. the other 40% was a mix between racist white people and non-racist white people.

I slipped up a little academically while I was there my freshman year, mainly due to me genuinely not caring about the classes. Essentially, the things that kept me a student there, were things my parents, loans and pockets weren't paying for. I was more interested in the fact that I was one of the students that were categorized in the 1% African Americans in the school. I was more interested in the fact that People really weren't coming together. My friend and I then started an organization on campus called PHILA, which means love, in which we had events and workshops to bring people together to celebrate and embrace each others differences.

As far as classes though, I just felt like I was being used for money. To me, a lot of colleges are just for profit. I was majoring in film and was payig my instructor to show me how to do things that

I have already learned to do the last 6 years of my life. He even jokingly mentioned that they should pay me to teach the class. I chuckled and left to change my major.

Then I ended up changing it two more times after that.

I'm currently not in school and i'm doing everything I want to do. I'm literally living the life that I want, just on a smaller level.

I would like to go back to school, maybe. I just don't want to feel like anyones statistic, anyones opportunity to make money off of or feel like I'm not being educated, or my time is being invested in something that doesn't truly invest in my future.

Maybe an art school? Those are too expensive. I'm not sure, but everything is not for everybody. If they really cared about our education, then money wouldn't stop a student from achieving their goals. Its should never be money, but #onlyinamaerica.

The root word of "Education" is "Educo," which means to "pull out"

Learning should want you to dig deep and pull out, learning should bring out your curiosity, pull out your creativity. We have too many teachers and not even educators. School Isn't about learning anymore, it's about passing.

Destiny Roberts

University of Wisconsin Stout

Dear Nisha,

I am exceptionally excited about graduating from college next year. I have grown so much and have become very independent over the last past three years of being in college. Moreover, I have acquired a few valuable experiences such as, studying more than I've ever had to before, getting a considerable amount of work experience, learning how to communicate effectively with others, and being responsible with decisions that will affect my future. These experiences have prepared me to move forward into the next chapter of my life. Although I am elated for this upcoming transition in my life, I am quite nervous because, I've never experienced life without school included (being that I went straight to college right after I graduated). The thing that I fear the most about graduating is acquiring a "career". My fear is to work a job JUST to make ends meet. Ultimately, I want to be financially stable, to be able to have a career that is enjoyable, and one that makes me happy. :)

Desiree Givan
Communications and Media Studies- Clayton State University

Dear Nisha,

I am vastly approaching my graduation date at Georgia State University with a Bachelor's of Social Work degree. As excited as I am, I also have several reservations. They are as follows:

- Will I find a job in my field? How long will the job hunting process take?
- Will I be making a decent amount of money from the job I land?
- Will I be able to maintain my own place to live?
- How will I be able to pay off my student loans?
- Will I be able to financially get my Master's?
- Should I wait before I go straight into my Master's to gain work experience?

As a social work major, I have had several social workers mention that it may take several jobs before finding the field in social work you are most passionate about in social work. Several areas interest me in my area of study, but what if I do not find my passion? What if I waste too much time switching jobs? What if I find out social work is not for me?

Also it is very common that graduates of any college or university have jobs/careers not related to their degrees at all. With the amount of money I had to use to pay for school, not finding a job in my field is unacceptable BUT what if it happens? I have never been at a point in my life where I did not know my next move. When I graduate, everything is up in the air in my case.

Help!

O.P.
Georgia State

Dear Branisha,

Graduating from college was probably one of the greatest accomplishments in my life. In addition to completing a life goal of mine I also made mom and dad proud (the fact that President Obama spoke at my graduation was also a plus). However, upon graduating I began to see what a lot of my peers were going through in regards to starting a career post-college. I had (and still do) a job working as a butcher at Kroger while I was trying to find better employment opportunities. I had an interview with ESPN when I graduated but wound up not getting the job. Eventually after several other interviews I began to question was I really good enough to get a job in the professional production field. Thankfully my family and friends got that idea out of my head very quick by reminding me of all the people I helped learn the craft while we were in school. And if they could find jobs then so could I, it just may take a little longer. With that in my head I went back to my campus job of working as the video coordinator for the Athletic department of morehouse. That was fun but I wasn't really making a lot of money BUT, I did gain valuable knowledge into what was needed if I wanted to do that job professionally. I stopped working for Morehouse in 2014 after the basketball season because the school did not have the budget to pay me. To make up for the income lost I took up my college hustle; photography and videography. I began doing photo shoots for various friends and customers in my store and reignited my passion for media. While it has been extremely tough to find a job in the field I know that God usually has a plan for everything and we each have our own journey in life. Knowing this is what kept me pushing forward even as all my friends around me were making big moves in life and in the careers and I was stuck in a grocery store. I stuck to my faith that my journey was the journey that

God had planned for me and they had their own journey. Eventually I wound up with a job as a school photographer for Lifetouch Photography but had to quit because they did not offer benefits and the work hours were long and hard. Following Lifetouch I got a night job as a security officer which I still have to this day, in addition to Kroger and my side phototography, making me work a grand total of three jobs (yikes). In a very fortunate/unfortunate turn of events I wound up in a car accident at the end of October and was forced to take time off work so I could heal. During the time that I have been on medical leave I have gained many new clients for photography and have secured contracts for events going into the new year. I have also taken the extra time to myself to sharpen my skills behind the lens and created a website to post my work. While I don't know what the year 2016 has in store for me, I'm ready to take it head on. I know that if I haven't given up on my dream of owning my own production company by now then there is still hope for me. I've never started a project I didn't finish so I guess there is motivation in that. Plus, I have God on my side and I know that He wont forsake me no matter what comes my way. If I had to tell someone in my shoes what to do, I would probably tell them that yes its hard, its damn hard, but nothing that is worth the struggle is going to come easy. Just keep pressing on, stay prayed up, HAVE FAITH IN YOURSELF AND YOUR ABILITIES (Lord knows I struggle with this one), and keep a good team of people around you.

Your Favorite Morehouse Man,

Cam

Dear Branisha,

Thank you for the opportunity to share pieces of my story. You are truly an inspiration to others, and I pray for your success with this book.

After graduation, I worked four different jobs during the interim before starting grad school. I graduated December 2009 and would not start grad school until August 2010. I ended my position with my alma mater's university bookstore, I worked for the Braves in guest relations (not as fancy as it sounds), and two positions through a staffing agency, O'Reileys shipping office and Carter's accounting office. I was so blessed to have these positions; however, because I battled physical and mental health, it was extremely difficult to see these blessings. It was difficult to keep my joy, and even more difficult to trust God. I constantly questioned Him asking why was *this chapter* a part of *my* journey. I gave so much energy to what seemed to me as my shortcomings and others' good fortune. *Life seemed so unfair!* Life was happening, and I couldn't cognitively process why things had become so bad for me. I thought I was a good person, knew I wasn't perfect, yet I could not understand what made me deserving of the things I endured.

I had lost all trust in God's word and desperately needed to regain my faith. I began praying and journaling, praying and fasting, praying and trusting. I continued this relationship through grad school, and found my time with God was the only thing that would satisfy my spiritual appetite. It was more important than the food I ate to feed my flesh. My soul was hungry, and I knew that Christ was all I needed to have joy and peace, two essentials for nourishing the soul.

Fast forward to adulting, since obtaining my master's degree, I have worked at two different higher education institutions, a community college and a university. Although my professional path altered, my professional goal did not. I have always wanted to be a steward to people, and by helping individuals with some of the most crucial decisions of their lives continues to rank #1 in my job satisfaction.

As an academic advisor, career counselor, and faculty member, I encourage students to seek resources and opportunities their college/university offers and take full advantage. As a person who has been in a mental space absence of faith and full of doubt, I encourage students to fully trust God. Use the gospel to feed your spirit and guide your steps. It is ok to be in a place of uncertainty, to not know what's next; but you should still be willing to learn, grow, and use your experiences as opportunities to discover your passion. Disregard status and prestige and focus on joy and peace. Your faith, diligence, and integrity will infinitely reveal how great and limitless He is in power. Take a day to rest, but keep going, keep working, and keep dreaming.

Your gifts will make room for you. - Proverbs 18:16

Sincerely,

Ashley Hixson

Founder of The Collegiate Voice
Ga. Southern

I returned, and saw under the sun, that the race *is* not to the swift, nor the battle to the strong, neither yet bread to the wise, nor yet riches to men of understanding, nor yet favour to men of skill; but time and chance happeneth to them all.

Ecc.9:11

Dear Branisha,

Let me 1st start off by saying I had no idea what I wanted to further my education in, so if you're the same as I was, your parents will decide for you. My parents selected business. Since I liked to talk, I then selected Marketing. I received my Bachelors in Business Administration in 2009! Now it was time to sale (market) myself to the tons of companies out there. Lucky enough for me I had been employed as a manager with Racetrac Petroleum, where my starting position was as an associate back in 2006. I started that job with no intention to stay nearly as much time as I had seen on my co- worker's name badges. I grew to love the company & the work I was doing so much that once I received my college diploma I applied to opportunities within Racetrac. I thought, "sure I know people already I'll just have to go through some formalities and I'll have the big job," BUT NOPE I got the TBNT (Thanks but No Thanks) , which blew my mind. I got my share of those responses before I finally got an offer as a Initial Trainer. Life after college was grand once this occurred I was successful.

Then came this nasty auntie of mine name " Struggle". No matter how successful anyone appears, everyone has been through the

Struggle. What help me out of my struggle most was relationship building & thats not taught in any curriculum out there. Life after college depends on you building strong/diverse relationships & worrying only about yourself & remembering to KISS (keep it simple stupid).

R.D.Neal

American Intercontinental University

Dear Branisha,

After college I pretty much got to the music. I started putting myself out there as a songwriter. I was inviting and booking artists to come to my home studio to work with me. I also worked with other songwriters and artists that were songwriters. Eventually I started going to known studios in Atlanta and meeting people that were set in the industry. I took a couple of trips back and forth to New York discussing business. Even though things were looking new to me, nothing was set just yet. I still grinded and acted as if nothing ever happened. I never splurged on who I knew or who I'd met. I always kept doing me. Also money was still tight. I was blessed to get to where I was by being paid for studio sessions from my home in the basement. So I say all this to say, you have to go after what you want. You have to tackle it head on. Sitting down waiting and saying I want or I wish I was is not going to feed you or reinvent your atmospheres. You have to work. That's just it in a nutshell. It might sound like this took 6months to a year to happen for me but it didn't!!!! It took like 5 years. Today I'm proud to say that I have over 100,000 views on vevo, a distribution deal through Warner Bros under MCR, my own app, a video on MTV and VH1, a book released, and preparing for the release of two albums. THATS WORK. I WORKED and I WORK. My advice is... Just do it, jump. Why not? You don't know where anything is gone come from, ain't nobody got all the answers. Can't nobody tell you the correct way to do nothing, all they can do is aim you in a direction where it's gone mess your mindset up, or make you keep going and work harder. I decided to do it for myself and be self-sufficient.

Yours Truly,

@ReyFonder

Dear Branisha,

Life after college was an interesting experience for me. For one I just got out of a serious relationship and things were still raw and painful. Going through that right after college was so hard. After leaving college, I had no direction at all. I was so lost and couldn't figure out what I wanted to do. I felt suffocated and unsure about everything. It was hard for me because I felt like everyone that I knew went and did things that they studied for. Moving back home was hard too because I didn't expect that I would be back home.

I decided to make a massive change about 2 months after graduation. I applied to a million jobs and didn't get any. This was the time when there was no jobs and finding a job was so competitive. I felt pretty worthless. So, I decided to take a massive leap of faith and move to Seattle. It felt good to be on my own again, but having no stable job made it so hard. For 6 months after graduation, I was stuck and even though I was in a different city, I felt like I was not doing anything. Which, to be honest, was the truth. I was working temp jobs and praying to just get an assignment. When I didn't, it was pretty rough.

I always thought that after graduating from college, I would have my career path set out for me and that I would be pretty settled down with a great job. That was not the case at all for me. I was in Seattle for about 5 months when I came upon an ad for teaching English in japan. I applied hoping to just get out of America and be away from all the unhappiness that I felt. For some reason, I was lucky and they accepted me.

I then moved back home for about 3 months and then I moved to Japan. Moving to Japan was like me running away. I was running away from my ex boyfriend. I was running away from not being able to find a job. I was running away from feeling useless and worthless. I was pretty much just running away from life itself.

I was praying that by being in a different country, I would be able to just kind of start fresh cause I knew no one. I could hopefully start over and figure out what to do with my life. Honestly, moving to japan, even though it started out with me running away from things, was one of the best decisions of my life. There comes a point in time where you just have to have a massive change. If things are stagnant, freshen it up with something exciting. If you feel like you are going at a snails pace, slide like no tomorrow. If you feel like the weight of the world is on your shoulder, carry it with a smile.

I went to Japan expecting it to be only for a year…but I actually stayed for 5 years. For the first 3 years, I was trying to figure out what I wanted to do in my life. Being in japan actually helped clear my mind and help me focus. After 3 years, I was able to find out what I love. I love planning and being around people. So, I took that passion and I decided to study project management.

After leaving japan, I am now at an amazing job working for a public high school promoting college education to students. It is amazing! I am actually helping kids realize their dreams. I am helping kids by showing them the options that they have to further their education!

So, if you look at it, life after college was tough. For me, it was tougher than most people. But now, after a couple of years, I realize that things are tough, but the toughness is what made me who I am and it made me a strong individual.

With Pleasure,

SV

University of Oregon

www.ingramcontent.com/pod-product-compliance
Lightning Source LLC
Chambersburg PA
CBHW072210090426
42740CB00012B/2470